Spanda Karika – Explained

Gateway to Nondual consciousness

By Achutha BK

Achutha BK
1st Edition

Publication Date: September 2024
Price: ₹220 | $ 11
ISBN: *978-93-5847-508-1*
Published by:
Adhyyan Books
Office No. 125,
Opposite Vivanta by Taj,
DDA SFS. Pocket-1, Dwarka,
Sec-22, New Delhi-110077
Website: http://adhyyanbooks.com
E-mail: contact@adhyyanbooks.com

Printed at: Repro Printers, Delhi

PREFACE

This is a reflection of author's journey. Osho's teaching taught - to surrender to existence. Existence is God. Call it "Astitva". Further Osho defined Tantra as total non-judgmental "acceptance". This was the beginning. Then came "Power of Now" by Eckhart Tolle, which is rooted in the "now" as a hint to carry on Osho's teachings.

Moved on to non-dual school of Shankara with many teachers. Existence is an illusion. It is only consciousness. Consciousness is the self-existing awareness. It is the first-person presence. Everything is consciousness. Everything happens in consciousness. This nondual truth allows worldly manifestations to rise and dissolve in consciousness. Science is moving towards accepting the illusion of the world as the right explanation.

How do we achieve this direct knowledge and realize "I am That"? Move on to Kashmir Shaivism. With limited exposure, it became evident. We need the world as a mirror of the same supreme consciousness to become aware. It is like we cannot see our own eyes and need a mirror. The reflected individual world and universe provides a mirror (with no outside object) to recognize its own "consciousness". It is like a gestalt of consciousness and its reflection (manifested world). Reflection is aware of consciousness. This is the possibility to recognize the "supreme consciousness" as the same as "individual consciousness" through reflection in the mirror (existence or world). The Supreme Consciousness, therefore, manifested into a world of ten thousand things. Each limited individuals have world of his own.

Thus, each individuals has a world. The non-dual consciousness wants to "play" and do not stay in singularity. The world helps the supreme consciousness to see and feel existence. The limited individuals, eyes and senses becomes the instruments of supreme consciousness. The beings though limited recognize the presence of the same infinite supreme consciousness in themselves. Now a returning journey is possible through existence (mirror) to see and feel first person (consciousness) without further regression intuitively. Spanda Karika in this book explains this return journey. Surrendering to "grace" for enabling to express as a book.

Love,

Achutha B.K.

CONTENTS

GURU VANDANA

Gurus include Rishi Prabhakar, Osho, Lao Tsu, Pande Ji, Nisarga Dutt Maharaj, Shankaracharya Ji (Shakatapuram), Rupert Spira, Echart Tolle and Tarneiv Ji.

On Kashmir Shaivism, Abhinava Gupta, Khemaraja, Jaideva Singh and Shiv Verma. This book has explanations as understood by author from gurus Jaideva Singh, Shiv Verma, Rupert Spira and others. Author is grateful to all.

ACKNOWLEDGEMENTS

Dr. Venkatesh Pai for actively listening to the reading of the book with author, Piyuush Kumaar to have worked hard to make the manuscript ready for publishing, the publisher of the book, Adhyyan Books and the complete team who made this possible.

Chapter-1
SWAROOPA SPANDA

VERSE-1

यस्योन्मेषनिमेषाभ्यां जगतः प्रलयोदयौ।
तं शक्तिचक्रविभवप्रभवं शङ्करं स्तुमः॥१॥

Yasyonmeṣanimeṣābhyāṁ Jagataḥ Pralayodayau |
Taṁ Śakticakravibhavaprabhavaṁ Śaṅkaraṁ Stumaḥ ||

EXPLANATION

Shiva through "swatantrya" creates unmesha (manifestation/ expression) and nimesha (concealment / dissolution) like opening of eye lid and closing of eye lid. This phenomenon is beyond time and space and thus have no sequence. With unmesha, "udaya" happens and with nimesha "pralaya" happens. Here the udaya and pralaya are sequential and bound by time and space. In unmesha shakti chakra of 12 gods of shakti which is joining and disjoining to create the world. Shakti chakra is the cause, and their joining & disjoining creates the world (like forces of gravitation, electromagnetic etc.). By lauding the Shankara which means by the grace of Shankara one enters finally Sada Shiva Tattva.

Insight:

Chitti is a phenomenon of non-dual Shiva consciousness. There is an activity in non-dual consciousness, "Kinchit Chalanam" like throb spanda - metaphor is a wriggling "serpent". This throb created by Shiva consciousness prakasha to create Iccha gives raise to shakti vimarsha. Vimarsha is required (like a mirror is required to see our own eyes) to reflect and know the prakasha, the awareness. Through vimarsha, one becomes aware of infinite awareness. This mirror does not have an outside object. The world we see is due to shakti created by throb in which the localized self with limited time and space is seen in the world. Each localized self sees its own world. The infinite awareness of Shiva consciousness needs this vimarsha of ten thousand localized beings to experience its own "leela" through vimarsha. Thus, there is prakasha, the light of non-dual consciousness with a gestalt like reflective world becoming aware of this awareness though vimarsha. The "intelligence" may need to see this world only through localized beings which are unmesha of the same consciousness and when the eye lid closes it conceals or dissolves to primordial consciousness. This macro spanda of Shiva-Shakti (prakasha and vimarsha) then gives rise to Iccha shakti, Gnana shakti and Kriya shakti. In Trika system, para, apara and parapara are the trika, the knower, the known and the knowing. Grace is the key to pratyabigna of re-recognizing that I am Shiva non-dual consciousness. So, we laud Shankara to enter Him by His grace and hence devotion is required.

VERSE-2

यत्र स्थितमिदं सर्वं कार्यं यस्माच्च निर्गतम्।
तस्यानावृतरूपत्वान्न निरोधोऽस्ति कुत्रचित्॥२॥

Yatra sthitamidaṁ sarvaṁ kāryaṁ yasmācca nirgata।
Tasyānāvṛtarūpatvānna nirodho'sti kutracit||2||

EXPLANATION

Here, we are resorting to Swaroopa Jnana from mangala shloka of Shiva consciousness with Shakti, we are discussing how one can attain spiritual clarity and elevate to get ready to enter Shiva consciousness.

Every worldly act starts with srishti (uttapatti / cretaion), laya (palana / maintenance) and samhara (dissolution). The verse says we see the world anavruta (means with no cover or veil). While we see shape and objects - for example when you see a golden necklace or an earring the gold is uncovered not veiled (anavruta). But we see the object in different shapes (akrutis) with doubtlessly made of gold which is also unveiled. Similarly, when we see a picture on a screen, we see the screen also on which the picture is being played. It is interesting to note that the content of the picture namely water does not wet the screen nor the fire in the picture burn the screen. Screen is always present with picture. This is "Tasya Anavruta Rupatwanna".

Now let us take our own thoughts. They are also like a picture on the screen. Thoughts are played on the mind; the mind must be trained for Swaroopa Jnana. The prakasha, the light illumines the thought or the event, it gives it a platform. This is what swaroopa does, gives it a platform and illumines. The "seer" only allows this platform for thought and illumines the thought to know. Key is not to get identified with this thought or event, the thought moves from creation to maintenance to dissolution. The seer just observes (nirodha), neither opposes nor accepts. Just allows the knowledge to pass by giving it prakasha (illumination) and platform (sthana).

Clarifications:

In the second line of the first verse can also be interpreted as below Shakti chakra is Srishti, laya i.e. palana and samhara. Here the seer abiding in itself, the journey is explained. The nature and recognition of seer are explained with practices. If any thought for example comes up, it is going through a cycle of uttapatti (creation), laya (maintenance) and samhara (dissolution). While this is going on, self or Swaroopa gives it a platform and illumines it (prakasha) till dissolution. On completion of the dissolution, the new thoughts get created. The mind (we will come to "self" later) witnesses without identification and practice happens. Anger, desire, sadness, joy etc. are thoughts that dries up and "self" gives it platform and illumines and understands through mind the rise and maintenance and dissolution of the thoughts or emotion. It is Stitha as mentioned in the second verse, there is no denial nor identification that means there is no denial or acceptance, it is pure nirodha. The owner of this is seer who is observing the creation, maintenance and dissolution of thought and it is his domain totally.

VERSE-3

जाग्रदादिविभेदेऽपि तदभिन्ने प्रसर्पति।
निवर्तते निजान्नैव स्वभावादुपलब्धृतः॥३॥

Jāgradādivibhede'pi tadabhinne prasarpati|
Nivartate nijānnaiva svabhāvādupalabdhṛtaḥ||3||

EXPLANATION

This refers to the state of waking, dreaming and sleeping. Seer is aware of these states but does not belong to these states. Seer experiences shedding prakasha (illumining these states) and understanding them by giving platform. But seer is only a drishta. The example is one can go in a day to three towns nearby he passes through them, he does not become them. Same way one knows the states is not the state himself. All these states are abhinna not broken that means one doesn't overlap the other. It is the nature or swabhava of seer to know these states. This is spanda principal. All the states are known to witness consciousness which is ever present as swabhava or spanda.

Some Practices

Practice:1

Choose a partner, allow a rehearsal of sorts. Let him create anger, humor or sadness in you as a prank. When you get identified with the corresponding emotion and forget the screen (knower or self) and react, pause and see to return to the screen. If it goes out of hands, stop it could be a political discussion also in the role playing.

Practice:2

Every half an hour check what was your awastha or state. Is it anger, sadness or happiness. Then look back at your true nature of screen not the picture and remove identity with picture. Patanjali says, "Yoga Chitta Vritti Nirodha". How to do it? "Abhyasa vairagyena chitta vriti nirodha, nirantara". Practice and renunciation continually will take you to the source. Source is the screen and allows to know the picture as a knower and provide a platform for the picture.

Rupert Spira gives a meditation to treat all emotions and objects in the foreground and remaining in the background of source. First move five minutes to experience the foreground (outer picture) then withdraw to source and watch the separate self. Practice is the key.

VERSE-4

अहं सुखी च दुःखी च रक्तश्चेत्यादिसंविदः।
सुखाद्यवस्थानुस्यूते वर्तन्तेऽन्यत्र ताः स्फुटम्॥४॥

Ahaṁ sukhī ca duḥkhī ca raktaścetyādisaṁvidaḥ|
Sukhādyavasthānusyūte vartante'nyatra tāḥ sphuṭam||4||

EXPLANATION

This verse defines Swaroopa or self with some dimensions of self. This is continuation with first three verses. It means, when we have a pleasant news or feel good, we are identified with sukha completely. Similarly, when dukha happens, we are sad, we also desire and hate (Ragadwesha). We also identify with relatives, friends at various points of time. All these states are pictures on the canvas but in each state the separate egoistic self-attaches and gets identified in this outworld journey.

For example – A wealthy person with all material comforts living abroad might become miserable with home sickness and want to return to near and dear ones. If a poor aspirant, gets result of becoming an IAS officer and gets a letter, his state changes to happiness though in reality it has not happened. It is like a nimitta, a tool. Like fire which causes the metal to be hot, the nature or swabhava of the metal is not high temperature. This is caused by the fire which has heat as its dharma, is the nimitta. The metal has dharma to be in room temperature. These states or avasthas drive us to identity, forgetting the self. These states or avasthas drive us to identity, forgetting the Self. Thus, the picture takes over and the screen is forgotten. The real Self is like staying on the screen and allow picture to play. Self is the owner. Knowing these states / avasthas (arise, maintain and dissolve), But the Self, the screen, remains unattached. That is, Anyatra Tahas Sputam.

VERSE-5

न दुःखं न सुखं यत्र न ग्राह्यं ग्राहकं न च।
न चास्ति मूढभावोऽपि तदस्ति परमार्थतः॥५॥

Na duḥkhaṁ na sukhaṁ yatra na grāhyaṁ grāhakaṁ na ca|
Na cāsti mūḍhabhāvo'pi tadasti paramārthataḥ||5||

EXPLANATION

We have been analyzing, who am I? First, we saw our mind illumines and provides platform and is also knower. Secondly, we moved from mind to seer knowing the mind creates identity with the picture on the screen. The picture like thought changes from sadness to happiness to humor etc. Mind accordingly is changing with identity. With Abhyasa and Vairagya we eliminate this identity by being a seer or the screen. We see that there are no veils around on what we see as dhrushya. We from a seer perspective learn to allow understanding, shedding prakasha and providing platform to thoughts, objects, desires etc. Passing the scene - dhrishya, to uttpati / creation, palana / maintenance and samahara / dissolution. Thus, we come up to screen the seer, untainted, but allowing objects and contents of consciousness of the world to rise and dissolve (ever-changing). Now with fifth verse we move beyond this seer concept to one of paramartha. Hence the real spanda is defined. The verse says you are not the enjoyer nor are you the sad one, nor the seer, nor the seen. You are not the jada (thing without Chaitanya), you are paramarthaha, spanda, who holds both seer and seen and its potential. You are the chaitanya.

Examples to understand – There is a great speaker who is waiting to speak. There are people waiting to listen. Even if the program is not done, the speaker has potential to express, and people are able to listen. Similarly, a poet is sleeping. His house catches fire and all poetry written are destroyed. But he has as a poet remains potential to write the poems again. So even without seer and seen, with grahya and grahaka, the self is shining. Same way these beings are not dumb, with (Mudabhave Api), they are all one divine spanda consciousness. This is easy to understand. Let us now dwell in Paramarthaha, take a table, we find its true nature is protons, neutrons, strings and waves, etc. It is energy or spanda or consciousness. There are three platforms in reality, which is one, Paramarthika platform, secondly, Prathibhasika platform, lastly Vyavaharika platform.

Take a table for example, its Paramarthika reality platform is energy, Spanda. Its Pratibhasika reality is wood. Its Vyavaharika reality is table. Similarly in beings, Vyavaharika being father, mother, son, Mohan, Suresh, etc. Pratibhasika reality is human beings or sentient beings. Paramarthika reality is energy, chaitanya, one infinite awareness of shared being and consciousness. This spanda principle therefore, after giving Swaroopalakshana, finally declares the real nature is Paramarthaha. Thus, the identity of the wave in the ocean is dropped and realizing it is the same nature as ocean, the separateness gets dropped. The real essence is water only. Same way, Rupert Spira says, we are all shared beings, the paramartha is infinite awareness, the essence being peace. Om Shanti.

VERSE-6

यतः करणवर्गोऽयं विमूढोऽमूढवत्स्वयम्।
सहान्तरेण चक्रेण प्रवृत्तिस्थितिसंहृतीः ॥६॥

Yataḥ karaṇavargo'yaṁ vimūḍho'mūḍhavatsvayam|
Sahāntareṇa cakreṇa pravṛttisthitisaṁhṛtīḥ||6||

VERSE-7

लभते तत्प्रयत्नेन परीक्ष्यं तत्त्वमादरात्।
यतः स्वतन्त्रता तस्य सर्वत्रेयमकृत्रिमा ॥७॥

Labhate tatprayatnena parīkṣyaṁ tattvamādarāt|
Yataḥ svatantratā tasya sarvatreyamakṛtrimā||7||

EXPLANATION

Moving deeper, we have instruments of body, mind, intellect (Yathaha Karana Vargo Ayam). These are instruments which are jada means inactive and lifeless and inert. They behave like Chaitanya, Consciousness when driven as instruments, Karana. They are otherwise dumb. Let us examine this further. All Indriyas act eating, drinking, touching and smelling. One acts, let's say, to eat a sweet, moves his hand to pick up and put in the mouth. Who is asking him to do it? It is the body; it is the mind. First level instruction comes from the mind to the body to act on Indriyas. Then let us say while the body is obeying the mind, intellect which is superior instrument to mind says, you are a diabetic, not supposed to eat sugar. The intellect decides and gives approval or rejection, and body obeys. So, we establish that the hierarchy of body action in mind first and then intellect is higher in command.

Let us move to subtler level. Let us see how the decision taken by the intellect buddhi gets reviewed either by acceptance or rejection by you (self). Only your strength finally agrees that the intellect has decided as final push is by you. Thus, you may still eat the sweet, though intellect has decided "no" on doctor's advice. Now you are able to talk to US on FaceTime from India. This happens due to having technology upakarana to transmit and capture images and voice spoken in US to India. These sound waves are spread all over and with right instruments can be captured. A satellite can send images of Earth in real time. Another example is Google Maps with traffic. The same limited consciousness, awareness, we used to accept or rejecting eating sweet is infinitely large and pervasive on examination. We restrict ourselves to a localized self and without practice gets limited. If we use our full potential, we can recognize we are all pervasive. Infinite awareness and one consciousness.

We can do the same things directly communicating and receiving sound waves and coo any place we want in real time like satellite image. A wave has to be recognized and acquire its original nature of a notion and come out of individual identity of wave. Space is in the pot which is like a localized should be broken open and merge with the space of the universe. Supreme Consciousness which nothing but you, same as your individual consciousness, once recognized, one has to just move attention to listen, see the complete universe without the need of any instrument like satellite receivers etc. Like you see with your inner eye, see a dream, one has the ability to be resting in infinite awareness. The consciousness is powerful like electricity driving all instruments like fan, bulb, heater, etc. Thus, we first examine the body, mind, intellect and consciousness.

"Labbate Tat Prayatnena Parikshyam Tat Tvam Adhrat", Once we realize an established tattva is as same as Infinite Awareness, Supreme Consciousness, we know it is svatantra and sarvatra and akrutima, totally independent, totally available in all and not artificial.

VERSE-8

न हीच्छानोदनस्यायं प्रेरकत्वेन वर्तते।
अपि त्वात्मबलस्पर्शात्पुरुषस्तत्समो भवेत्॥८॥

Na hīcchānodanasyāyaṁ prerakatvena vartate|
Api tvātmabalasparśātpuruṣastatsamo bhavet||8||

EXPLANATION

The Karana-varga, (the instruments of individual consciousness) namely body, mind, intellect, desire, etc. seem to be acting on their own. The body and indriyas operate only after there is a touch from your consciousness. Your inside self-touches and agrees or rejects a said action of a body which has hierarchy of mind, intellect. But the strength comes from individual consciousness as explained in the next verse. Though we feel as if the desire is acting through karana vargas, it is finally the touch of consciousness and its svikruti (acceptance). Example, if we are walking 10 rounds in the garden, goal being 10 rounds, health advice being 10 rounds, we see around and decide to stop at the 8th round. If we are cheating ourselves, when you examine, the stop decision comes from touching the consciousness, though we feel guilty.

VERSE-9

निजाशुद्ध्यासमर्थस्य कर्तव्येष्वभिलाषिणः।
यदा क्षोभः प्रलीयेत तदा स्यात्परमं पदम्॥९॥

Nijāśuddhyāsamarthasya kartavyeṣvabhilāṣiṇaḥ|
Yadā kṣobhaḥ pralīyeta tadā syātparamaṁ padam||9||

EXPLANATION

In the last verse we understood that we touch the consciousness (atmabala), and still do not realize the full potential and strength available with operating from consciousness. We always behave like localized beings with limitation and are unable to experience our own divine consciousness. To be resting and operating from consciousness we have infinite strength and limitless awareness. We are not able to realize our "self" is limitless, changeless, profound infinite awareness. Why? This is due to ashuddha covering or veil we have on the self. It is like an impurity. We do not get connected to the source just like a battery full of power has a plastic lid on top insulating it. Till this is removed or our veil is removed. We are limited and ignorant of the power of self.

What causes this veil or impurity? The second line of the verse explains this impurity or veil is due to identity. We attach to ourselves like somebody father, son, mother, Hindu, Muslim, carpenter, mason etc. Once the identity is dropped the space in the pot breaks, the pot merges with infinite space or awareness. Thus by dropping identity, self relises limitless being and its infinite awareness.

VERSE-10

तदास्याकृत्रिमो धर्मो ज्ञत्वकर्तृत्वलक्षणः।
यतस्तदेप्सितं सर्वं जानाति च करोति च॥१०॥

Tadāsyākṛtrimo dharmo jñatvakartṛtvalakṣaṇaḥ|
Yatastadepsitaṁ sarvaṁ jānāti ca karoti ca||10||

EXPLANATION

The limited, localized being will merge with infinite awareness. The small I, the limited Ahamta merges with big I, the infinite consciousness. When this kshudra, (limited small I), Aham is dropped and immersed in natural Dharma (swabhava), then infinite knowledge and capacity to "do" is naturally achieved. A limited being understands and does in a limited way whatever is happening to his body, for example, any part of his body is itching, he will realize, understand and act. Similarly, all the understanding and actions from Kshudra Ahamta, limited small I, are localized. Once this transformation of real nature of Self is revealed, one has access to infinite understanding and actions.

A practice by Rupert Spira - Feel the sensation in the eyelids. Go deep and see where is this experienced, it is in your awareness. Where the sensation is experienced? Move to the resting of hand on the chair, experience the sensation. You will find again inside you on the screen of awareness, the experience. Let the sensation leave the body. What happens? Now try when your son or daughter calls home in India from US, he or she has met with an accident and in deep pain. You are likely to experience on your screen of awareness that pain for a short time. If we remove the veil, Ashuddha, Kshudra, Ahamta, and see openly, we have infinite awareness to understand the whole and act on the whole by mere attention. We must understand we are infinite beings and the whole universe we are present once we have understanding Gnana of the spreading and merging with Big I, we need practice.

We need to accept and surrender in this practice of ending dualism or separation by understanding the Gnana which is infinite can also be used to manifest actions. This svikruti or surrender needs to be practiced. At body level if we bite our tongue, we do not blame the teeth. They are both same. The body except the teeth that bit the tongue is okay and moves on. Thus, life, then family, wife, son and daughter become acceptable. In the same way the whole brahmanda is the same consciousness of self will be realized on surrender, the divisiveness does not appear. It is like an egoistic wave merge and loses the identity in the ocean and accepts it is the whole ocean and is tattva of water. Similar realization allows the merging into self and resulting in merging into the big I, the supreme consciousness. We will be shared beings with peace. All manifestations are from Spanda. Hence all the matter and beings return to the Spanda. We know a table or a fan or a car are finally energy. They are all protons, neutrons and electrons or waves or strings, but finally same energy is expressed.

VERSE-11

तमधिष्ठातृभावेन स्वभावमवलोकयन्।
स्मयमान इवास्ते यस्तस्येयं कुसृतिः कुतः॥११॥

Tamadhiṣṭhātṛbhāvena svabhāvamavalokayan|
Smayamāna ivāste yastasyeyaṁ kusṛtiḥ kutaḥ||11||

EXPLANATION

This verse explains the experience of divinity, self-awareness and self-realization. Once one stablishes in the source (abiding in self), the experience the swabhava or nature of things and world one realizes he is in everything and everything is in him. Like he realizes the world is made up of particles, neutrons, protons, electrons, and waves, and strings, and is emanating from energy, and it is the same in him and everywhere in the manifested world. He cannot take any lower position while dealing with the world. It is like a wave established in its source, knows that it is the same ocean and other waves made up of water. With this vismaya revelation, the self sees its expansion and enters into non-dual infinite awareness / consciousness.

VERSE-12

नाभावो भाव्यतामेति न च तत्रास्त्यमूढता।
यतोऽभियोगसंस्पर्शात्तदासीदिति निश्चयः॥१२॥

Nābhāvo bhāvyatāmeti na ca tatrāstyamūḍhatā|
Yato'bhiyogasaṁsparśāttadāsīditi niścayaḥ||12||

EXPLANATION

Buddhists deal with void in the swaroopa in the being and seer as void leading to shoonya (Swaroopa) like we see a picture on screen and the absence of picture the screen is still "seen", same way if people are sitting on a dais, it is seen and in the absence of people still the dais is seen. Our true nature is to illumine (understand and provide the platform. This is done in abhava or when the content of consciousness is void. Still the swaroopa (self is vibrant) and illumines and provides stance. Let us see in the following examples. In Sushupti sleep state, the self, the individual (individual consciousness small and limited I), is shining and providing platform. It understand if the sleep was deep enough or not. Secondly, in Samadhi, during nirvikalp samadhi, the self is aware of going into samadhi and returning to jagrat avastha. The self is available in all states to understand and shine and provide platform. In all states or avasthas including abhava state, the state of void, the seer in the self is watching, giving prakasha. It is important to note that while above process of experiencing bhava and abhava provides the same seer experiencing in both states, providing prakasha and platform, at the same time the self when experiencing svabhava is vibrant and not jada, inanimate. You are the vibrant self.

VERSE-13

अतस्तत्कृत्रिमं ज्ञेयं सौषुप्तपदवत्सदा।
न त्वेवं स्मर्यमाणत्वं तत्तत्त्वं प्रतिपद्यते॥१३॥

Atastatkṛtrimaṁ jñeyaṁ sauṣuptapadavatsadā|
Na tvevaṁ smaryamāṇatvaṁ tattattvaṁ pratipadyate||13||

EXPLANATION

This verse is a culmination of previous one. The abhava state we witness, which we illumine and provide platform is known as changing nature, krutimaa and we can experience it and understand this void appearing and dissolving to the next state or thought. For example, we are aware with shining and stance during all the three states of waking, dreaming and sleeping state. (Sushupti -abhava state) We also similarly witness samadhi state. Like the eyes cannot see itself, the self also does not go back to see itself. The going beyond to watch / witness stops at "self", swaroopa. Its nature like eyes, can see, to illumine and provide a platform is the end all.

We therefore are not voids but that principle of swaroopa shining and allowing its awareness, contents of consciousness including abhava or void. These experiences cannot be recollected from memory. The state of sleep or Samadhi can be remembered. This is not the character of Spanda principle or Atma "self", it is always the experient, the knower, the cognizer. While admitting shoonya as a state, spanda does not agree that it is a final reality. Spanda says experient and subject cannot be brought to the level of object. It is consciousness itself which has all the states passing through it, its string, including Sushupti and Shoonya (void). This subject experient is the light that makes all appearances possible (katoupanishad).

VERSE-14

अवस्थायुगलं चात्र कार्यकर्तृत्वशब्दितम्।
कार्यता क्षयिणी तत्र कर्तृत्वं पुनरक्षयम्॥१४॥

Avasthāyugalaṁ cātra kāryakartṛtvaśabditam|
Kāryatā kṣayiṇī tatra kartṛtvaṁ punarakṣayam||14||

EXPLANATION

This verse continues to describe Swaroopa, (Self). There are two aspects, one the knower and the other is known. The known is ever changing, like one has a desire today or a goal, he creates it, maintains it and dissolves it. By doing so he gives rise to another desire, (sankalpa). Again, the same cycle, the knower unchangingly shines and illumines the understanding and provides the platform to know. But it remains changeless as the object or content keeps undergoing change of utpatti, palana and samhara. Thus, the knower and known, or doer and the deed are related. The deed keeps changing like the picture on the screen. The screen the knower or seer remains changeless.

VERSE-15

कार्योन्मुखः प्रयत्नो यः केवलं सोऽत्र लुप्यते।
तस्मिँल्लुप्ते विलुप्तोऽस्मीत्यबुधः प्रतिपद्यते॥१५॥

Kāryonmukhaḥ prayatno yaḥ kevalaṁ so'tra lupyate|
Tasmim̐llupte vilupto'smītyabudhaḥ pratipadyate||15||

EXPLANATION

This verse deals with three types of beings. One is realized being Gnani, abides in the Self, the second one is a seeker who is on direct progressive path, (Prabuddha) and the third category, a normal Abuddha, or ignorant being. When the outside world demands and seeks action, there is confirmation that I am doing the work. The realization of the presence is felt in abuddha, (ignorant) also. But when work is over and nothing to do, he does not remain present and gets into a shell as if he is not there. The other categories realize that when work is complete, they are still awake and aware and shine in non-doing as well.

For example, a speaker gives a talk outwardly, using senses and acts in the world. But after and before the talk, he is fully filled with chaitanya and potential of lecturing and imparting knowledge. Same way the potential is always present in the Prabuddha and Gnani. It is like you have a book in front of you, you are getting knowledge reading it as a knower. The object is known. When book is not there, you are still a knower. Same way you eat food in front of you as a doer and enjoyer. But even when in its absence the ability remains. If we are working outwards through senses or cease to work, we have no doubt about our presence, our swaroopa in the Gnatha (knower) and Bhogta (enjoyer) at all times including during absence of activity or work.

VERSE-16

न तु योऽन्तर्मुखो भावः सर्वज्ञत्वगुणास्पदम्।
तस्य लोपः कदाचित्स्यादन्यस्यानुपलम्भनात्॥१६॥

Na tu yo'ntarmukho bhāvaḥ sarvajñatvaguṇāspadam|
Tasya lopaḥ kadācitsyādanyasyānupalambhanāt||16||

EXPLANATION

When we turn into inner journey, we reach our normal state of being. This gives us what is called normal (samaya) pervasive state (know all state). Let us understand with example, when water which is operating separately as an entity (vishishta) in an ocean makes an inward journey to achieve the normal pervasive state which shows all wave are water. And all reside in the ocean full of water. Similarly, when one drops outwardly actions (vruttis) and turns inwards one reaches normal pervasive state of sarvaganatva gunaspandam (know all states).

In this state there is no residue. Tasya lopah kadachitsyad - nothing left incomplete. If there is now water or ocean there is no question of existence of wave. Thus, all vruttis including individual identity is illumined by spanda (normal pervasive state, Swaroopa, self). Spanda creates this normal state which is realized by normal state.

VERSE-17

तस्योपलब्धिः सततं त्रिपदाव्यभिचारिणी।
नित्यं स्यात्सुप्रबुद्धस्य तदाद्यन्ते परस्य तु॥१७॥

Tasyopalabdhiḥ satataṁ tripadāvyabhicāriṇī|
Nityaṁ syātsuprabuddhasya tadādyante parasya tu||17||

EXPLANATION

In this verse there is distinction of Prabuddha and Suprabuddha. From an initiation and teaching perspective, the one who is Suprabuddha (Gnani realized), is abiding in Self, (source and the screen), in all three states of waking, sleeping and dreaming. All the time, his inner nature uninterruptedly shines, identical with Shiva. Whereas Prabuddha is recognizing the states of dreaming and sleeping as his kingdom, which shines in those two states from Chaitanya. But in the waking state and Turiya state he is not recognizing fully the Chaitanya. Another way to explain this is Prabuddha partially enlightened (can only feel beginning and ending of these three states namely waking, dreaming and sleeping).

VERSE-18

ज्ञानज्ञेयस्वरूपिण्या शक्त्या परमया युतः।
पदद्वये विभुर्भाति तदन्यत्र तु चिन्मयः॥१८॥

Jñānajñeyasvarūpiṇyā śaktyā paramayā yutaḥ|
Padadvaye vibhurbhāti tadanyatra tu cinmayaḥ||18||

EXPLANATION

Here in this verse the four states are categorized waking and dreaming state in one category, the sleeping and Turiya states in the second category. In waking and dreaming state there is a knower and a known or Gnana knowledge and Gneya known. The difference in the waking state, outer sensory perceptions organs are active and dream state it is activeness in subtle sensory perceptions (organs). In the second category in sleep state there is merging state into Karana, (maya) of self. This is like electricity which is giving power to various equipment like bulb heater, refrigerator or different colors of the bulbs merge into the potential of electricity when switched off. The switching off is the sushupti or deep sleep state. The knower, the knowable is absorbed similar state like switched off electricity. There is a common experience on waking of Upalabdhi/ Attaining. There is a common experience on waking Upalabdhi (attaining sound sleep). This experience is same or common to all beings there is no knower and known phenomena like first category only consciousness is present. In Turiya state the difference is the knower abides in the self and experiences it is the same consciousness in all jivas. The electricity which is present, when switched off, is aware, it is the same electricity which works on bulb, heater, refrigerator. These equipment or appliances or jivas carrying the same shared consciousness is realized in "turia" state.

VERSE-19

गुणादिस्पन्दनिष्यन्दाः सामान्यस्पन्दसंश्रयात्।
लब्धात्मलाभाः सततं स्युर्ज्ञस्यापरिपन्थिनः॥१९॥

Guṇādispandaniṣyandāḥ sāmānyaspandasaṁśrayāt|
Labdhātmalābhāḥ satataṁ syurjñasyāparipanthinaḥ||19||

EXPLANATION

Let us understand this verse with some examples. The wave in an ocean has an identity and looks separate but its nature is water, (salty etc.) is same and is dependent on the nature of ocean. Similarly, the pictures on the screen have different identity. The pictures depend on the same screen to exhibit them. This source is svabhava and samanya spanda. The gunas namely rajas, tamas and sattvik are vruttis like anger, sadness etc. are all like identities which are dependent on the svabhava or nature of samanya spanda. The gunas are continuously dependent on samanya spanda. A wave is always dependent on ocean all the time for its existence. Same way, a screen is continually required for pictures to be projected on. Thus, the gunas flow and attain identity from the same, generic spanda. The Gnani or Suprabuddha knows the source as generic spanda and remain unaffected in his Swaroopa (self), as he remains in this truth, that all this emanates from his own source.

VERSE-20

अप्रबुद्धधियस्त्वेते स्वस्थितिस्थगनोद्यताः।
पातयन्ति दुरुत्तारे घोरे संसारवर्त्मनि॥२०॥

Aprabuddhadhiyastvete svasthitisthaganodyatāḥ|
Pātayanti duruttāre ghore saṁsāravartmani||20||

EXPLANATION

Suprabuddha established in self. Lets gunas namely tamas, rajas and sattvik flow and is not identified with them and abides in samaya spanda. The aprabuddha identifies with gunas and behaves the way the gunas and vruttis rise in him. He is always in the veil and not able to see his swaroopa (spanda). Aprabuddha does not look beyond the body mind and thoughts. He identifies with them with gunas and accordingly becomes sukkhi or dukkhi. Thus, the Aprabuddha falls into the samsara and worldly affairs by thus identifying with body mind and intellect and acting as per their conditioning and experiencing, the challenges of samsara and the aprabuddha is limited. He does not know the infinite potential of his (self) is unrealized and, once realized like a Gnani or Surabuddha, can understand and act in whole universe being one with Godhood.

VERSE-21

अतः सततमुद्युक्तः स्पन्दतत्त्वविविक्तये।
जाग्रदेव निजं भावमचिरेणाधिगच्छति॥२१॥

Ataḥ satatamudyuktaḥ spandatattvaviviktaye|
Jāgradeva nijaṁ bhāvamacireṇādhigacchati||21||

EXPLANATION

This verse concludes the jivanmukta state for the Gnani or Prabuddha. By constantly abiding being mindful of Spanda, (Self), one enters the Shankara, the Shiva consciousness. All the verses points to attaining this everlasting presence in Spanda to enter Shankara consciousness and be a jivanmukta. Though the Gnani or Suprabuddha attains the state of oneness and being everywhere and in everything. Recognizing "that" which he is, happens due to grace and devotion.

VERSE-22

अतिक्रुद्धः प्रहृष्टो वा किं करोमीति वा मृशन्।
धावन्वा यत्पदं गच्छेत्तत्र स्पन्दः प्रतिष्ठितः॥२२॥

Atikruddhaḥ prahṛṣṭo vā kiṁ karomīti vā mṛśan|
Dhāvanvā yatpadaṁ gacchettatra spandaḥ pratiṣṭhitaḥ||22||

EXPLANATION

This verse explains how to recognize spaṇḍa, the source in waking state. Vignana Bhairava Tantra gives methods to do this by observing the breath at the small gap of inhale and exhale or between two thoughts to catch spanda moment of observing silence between sounds or while going to sleep catching the moment of sleep by being aware of the transition. Here the Karika says when an extreme emotion of anger or joy erupts when one loses control, the Spanda moment appears if one is alert to observe it with introspection. The source is revealed in extreme conditions as veils are dropped and Spanda can be grasped. The next level of energy is felt in adventure sports like bungee jumping, mountaineering and various moments of exhaustion also. Even in the moments of fear, a person who is this Aprabuddha is stunned and might feel numb. Alert Gnani can use this to experience the source, the throb, the Spanda.

VERSE-23

यामवस्थां समालम्ब्य यदयं मम वक्ष्यति।
तदवश्यं करिष्येऽहमिति सङ्कल्प्य तिष्ठति॥२३॥

Yāmavasthāṁ samālambya yadayaṁ mama vakṣyati|
Tadavaśyaṁ kariṣye'hamiti saṅkalpya tiṣṭhati||23||

EXPLANATION

This verse is a turning point. So far, we had swaroopagnana, understanding self with practices as instructed. Now is the verse to abide in self or spanda. There is dropping of the separate self, the gunas, the vruttis, the thoughts, the actions etc. Now to surrender to the "supreme self" and act as "that" is acting in resonance. It is actually end of sankalpa. Man, buddhi, chit, ahankara all are dropped. Complete separate self or veil is dropped. The avastha state to which the surrendering has happened till this verse is the state to which I surrender now and completely move and act according to the spanda tattva. As the state I have surrendered to is supreme. Here depending on (ashraya) on this I surrender all sankalpas and just resonate with the guidance from supreme consciousness dissolving the separate self.

VERSE-24

तामाश्रित्योर्ध्वमार्गेण चन्द्रसूर्यावुभावपि।
सौषुम्नेऽध्वन्यस्तमितो हित्वा ब्रह्माण्डगोचरम्॥२४॥

Tāmāśrityordhvamārgeṇa candrasūryāvubhāvapi|
Sauṣumne'dhvanyastamito hitvā brahmāṇḍagocaram||24||

EXPLANATION

When yogi surrenders or drops mind, intellect, ego, separate self, his yogic chemistry changes. This is described in this verse. He is now abiding in the consciousness. The process is that energy or prana which was in Ida, Chandra or Somanadi or Pingala or Prananadi gets upward motion into the Sushumna Nadi. This penetration which happens due to surrender of Gunas and Vruttis and dropping the veil of separate self allows Yogi his infiniteness in consciousness. Yogi to experience his infiniteness in consciousness, (Brahmanda Gocharam). He is able to experience and transcend space and time.

VERSE-25

तदा तस्मिन्महाव्योम्नि प्रलीनशशिभास्करे।
सौषुप्तपदवन्मूढः प्रबुद्धः स्यादनावृतः॥२५॥

Tadā tasminmahāvyomni pralīnaśaśibhāskare|
Sauṣuptapadavanmūḍhaḥ prabuddhaḥ syādanāvṛtaḥ||25||

EXPLANATION

This way the sun and moon get covered, dissolved in Brahmanda by merging within the cosmos. Praleena means getting merged as one. The muda, aprabuddha, the ignorant treats this phenomenon as to shushupti, sleep state. The prabuddha catches glimpse of spanda, this moment of merging. Verse 23, 24 and 25, once the Suprabuddha yogi established in infinite awareness consciousness, he is continuously alert in the spanda state merged with supreme consciousness in all states of waking, dreaming and sleeping. The ignorant or aprabuddha is either stupefied or in deep sleep or sushupti.

Chapter-2

SAHAJA VIDYODAYA SPANDA

VERSE-26

तदाक्रम्य बलं मन्त्राः सर्वज्ञबलशालिनः।
प्रवर्तन्तेऽधिकाराय करणानीव देहिनाम्॥॥

Tadākramya balaṁ mantrāḥ sarvajñabalaśālinaḥ|
Pravartante'dhikārāya karaṇānīva dehinām||26||

EXPLANATION

This is a new section. Up to 25 verses, Swaroopa-spanda is revealed. In the final verse, the separate self, veil is dropped, and yogi establishes and abides in the self and is merged with infinite awareness. This section goes further to rise the innate knowledge which shows that consciousness is all persuasive. The above verse is describing a yogi abiding in self after surrendering gunas and vruttis can provide a mantra which can manifest in the real world as per the sankalpa of mantra. The mantra is just on paper and has no impact unless it arises from the inner atmabala (strength of yogi) and is from Spanda. This has authority to work through senses and the world and fructify the desired impact of mantra. Only a Suprabuddha (realized yogi) can deliver this. Otherwise, they are just words on paper.

VERSE-27

तत्रैव सम्प्रलीयन्ते शान्तरूपा निरञ्जनाः।
सहाराधकचित्तेन तेनैते शिवधर्मिणः॥२७॥

Tatraiva sampralīyante śāntarūpā nirañjanāḥ|
Sahārādhakacittena tenaite śivadharmiṇaḥ||27||

EXPLANATION

The mantras which have emerged are from Spanda principle. They carry the duties assigned to them and attain Shantarupa, thus ceasing the action, and are dissolved into Spanda principle or Shiva principle. This return happens with the knowledge of devoted people (the target experient). This is Shuddha Vidya, manifestation and dissolution happens, it is also the platform for functioning of mantra. These are the powers of a realized yogi, after surrendering the separate self, can produce.

VERSE-28

यस्मात्सर्वमयो जीवः सर्वभावसमुद्भवात्।
तत्संवेदनरूपेण तादात्म्यप्रतिपत्तितः॥॥

Yasmātsarvamayo jīvaḥ sarvabhāvasamudbhavāt|
Tatsaṁvedanarūpeṇa tādātmyapratipattitaḥ||28||

EXPLANATION

The localized limited self-experiences his local world as all entities arise in him. Thus, he identifies himself with world object and thought. Therefore, all the states, individual self-experiences in Shiva. So, the experiencer abides in the experienced. It is divine himself who is experiencer also dwelling in the field of experienced. This opens the scope to recognize the Jiva to expand to Shiva the divine non-dual consciousness. Both are same. It is only through Jiva after the Leela in the world, the infinite consciousness is realized as same. Jiva and Shiva are the journey through knowing, known and knower. Jiva is the only experiencer available to realize Shiva.

VERSE-29

तस्माच्छब्दार्थचिन्तासु न सावस्था न या शिवः।
भोक्तैव भोग्यभावेन सदा सर्वत्र संस्थितः॥॥

Tasmācchabdārthacintāsu na sāvasthā na yā śivaḥ|
Bhoktaiva bhogyabhāvena sadā sarvatra saṁsthitaḥ||29||

EXPLANATION

Explaining further everything in the world, Jiva experiences is Shiva. In fact, the world is in him as non-dual consciousness and is reflection of the same world inside which appears as a reflection in a limited Jiva. Therefore, all worlds, all narratives and all avastas of this experience is Shiva roopa only. Same way an enjoyer one fulfills the desire through object of enjoyment like eating of a sweet, is also emanating from the enjoyer and returns to the enjoyer while experience is also enjoyer only as the world that is out there as object of eating is recalling of a reflection of the limited self in the localized world. The expansion one has to see that the knower, known and knowing are inside an infinite awareness will be through this world projected by the self. Thus, the wave in the sea is due to sea and it is all water so is all Shiva tattva of infinite sea. The wave appears in the world as Shiva tattva and dissolves into the ocean. Therefore, world is inside the consciousness and gets expressed prakasha and vimarsha. Another example could be the picture comes with screen and is integral with it. Wave is integral to the ocean and gold is integral to the different ornaments. Experiencer is the Experienced.

VERSE-30

इति वा यस्य संवित्तिः क्रीडात्वेनाखिलं जगत्।
स पश्यन्सततं युक्तो जीवन्मुक्तो न संशयः॥॥

Iti vā yasya saṁvittiḥ krīḍātvenākhilaṁ jagat|
Sa paśyansatataṁ yukto jīvanmukto na saṁśayaḥ||30||

EXPLANATION

In this verse, the yogi has realized and abides in Self, realizing he is Shiva Consciousness and the world he experiences is also Shiva consciousness. He has surrendered his separate self of Raga, Dvesha and Vruttis ego, body, mind and is in infinite awareness. The small I has merged with big I. He therefore interacts with world as “Krida” or “play” and is liberated while alive (Jeevan Mukta). This is beyond doubt.

VERSE-31

अयमेवोदयस्तस्य ध्येयस्य ध्यायिचेतसि।
तदात्मतासमापत्तिरिच्छतः साधकस्य या॥॥

Ayamevodayastasya dhyeyasya dhyāyicetasi|
Tadātmatāsamāpattiricchataḥ sādhakasya yā||31||

EXPLANATION

The verse declares that the object of meditation in the meditator's mind is the Shiva consciousness (light of non-duality, Spanda). This is so because the manifestation which brings about the identity of the meditator with that of object of meditation. All words, objects or thoughts are Shiva's state as there is nothing else other than Shiva tattva. The identity with Shiva is not some other perception nor determination, but it is a non-ideated, deep will of entering to be one with Shiva consciousness.

VERSE-32

इयमेवामृतप्राप्तिरयमेवात्मनो ग्रहः।
इयं निर्वाणदीक्षा च शिवसद्भावदायिनी॥॥

Iyamevāmṛtaprāptirayamevātmano grahaḥ|
Iyaṁ nirvāṇadīkṣā ca śivasadbhāvadāyinī||32||

EXPLANATION

This alone is drinking of nectar leading to immortality. This alone is self-realization. This alone is the deeksha, initiation to Shiva consciousness.

The second section of Sahaja Vidyodaya ends here. This reaffirms all that is in the world, the experienced is the same non-dual Shiva consciousness. There is only one identity of oneness that is big I. Supreme consciousness that runs through all reality. Everything is Shiva.

Chapter-3
VIBHUTI SPANDA

VERSE-33

यथेच्छाभ्यर्थितो धाता जाग्रतोऽर्थान् हृदि स्थितान्।
सोमसूर्योदयं कृत्वा सम्पादयति देहिनः॥ ॥

Yathecchābhyarthito dhātā jāgrato'rthān hṛdi sthitān|
Somasūryodayaṁ kṛtvā sampādayati dehinaḥ||33||

VERSE-34

तथा स्वप्नेऽप्यभीष्टार्थान्प्रणयस्यानतिक्रमात्।
नित्यं स्फुटतरं मध्ये स्थितोऽवश्यं प्रकाशयेत्॥ ॥

Tathā svapne'pyabhīṣṭārthānpraṇayasyānatikramāt|
Nityaṁ sphuṭataraṁ madhye sthito'vaśyaṁ prakāśayet||34||

EXPLANATION

This verse can be understood with deeper meaning. The non-dual Shiva consciousness, from its singularity, enters the body of Yogi and fulfills all desires abiding in the heart of Yogi. This is like an infinite awareness of Shiva experiencing the world through his own created being (instrument) of limited senses. The Yogi is awake in the waking state and is aware it is the same infinite consciousness that he is. The yogi thus awakened with entering of the consciousness in the body can cause the rise of moon and sun. By being aware of the moment between waking and sleeping transition, a gap is available the supreme reality for a yogi. He thus gains dreams to happen under his control. The Shiva consciousness being in sushumna (central naadi) makes this dream of desired or willed to reveal vividly. Thus, the inner sincerity of yogi is blessed with grace and the above experience of yogi happens in waking, dreaming and sleep states.

VERSE-35

अन्यथा तु स्वतन्त्रा स्यात्सृष्टिस्तद्धर्मकत्वतः।
सततं लौकिकस्येव जाग्रत्स्वप्नपदद्वये॥॥

Anyathā tu svatantrā syātsṛṣṭistaddharmakatvataḥ|
Satataṁ laukikasyeva jāgratsvapnapadadvaye||35||

EXPLANATION

The previous verse experiences in Jagrat and Swapna (dream), manifest only when the prayer of Yogi is blessed by the grace. Thus, the divinity enters. It is the Swatantra or freedom of divine consciousness to bestow this grace to Yogi as described in the previous verse. The verse confirms, during all other times, there is no difference to the experience of Yogi or other beings in both waking and dreaming states. It is the usual experience of world while in awake and dream world.

VERSE-36

यथा ह्यर्थोऽस्फुटो दृष्टः सावधानेऽपि चेतसि।
भूयः स्फुटतरो भाति स्वबलोद्योगभावितः॥॥

Yathā hyartho'sphuṭo dṛṣṭaḥ sāvadhāne'pi cetasi|
Bhūyaḥ sphuṭataro bhāti svabalodyogabhāvitaḥ||36||

VERSE-37

तथा यत्परमार्थेन येन यत्र यथा स्थितम्।
तत्तथा बलमाक्रम्य न चिरात्सम्प्रवर्तते॥॥

Tathā yatparamārthena yena yatra yathā sthitam|
Tattathā balamākramya na cirātsampravartate||37||

EXPLANATION

Things may look unclear and distant even when one sees it with an attentive mind first. But yogi exercises his innate nature, spanda power. Then the thing in any form or place or time manifests vividly with full clarity. Yogi is the powerful instrument of Supreme Consciousness to its experience of its own manifested world instantly through the cleansed instrument which has acquired to abide in self same as infinite awareness.

VERSE-38

दुर्बलोऽपि तदाक्रम्य यतः कार्ये प्रवर्तते।
आच्छादयेद्बुभुक्षां च तथा योऽतिबुभुक्षितः॥॥

Durbalo'pi tadākramya yataḥ kārye pravartate|
Ācchādayedbubhukṣāṁ ca tathā yo'tibubhukṣitaḥ||38||

EXPLANATION

A person who is weak and incapable of work to be done can achieve results and success by the power of spanda. Similarly, a hungry or thirsty person can fulfill himself. Similarly, one who is sorrowful and or delusional or suffering from old age or death (of the body) can also accomplish positive outcomes. The spanda drives all this to the end of accomplishment. By and by, the very spanda gets revealed to beings.

VERSE-39

अनेनाधिष्ठिते देहे यथा सर्वज्ञतादयः।
तथा स्वात्मन्यधिष्ठानात्सर्वत्रैवं भविष्यति॥॥

Anenādhiṣṭhite dehe yathā sarvajñatādayaḥ|
Tathā svātmanyadhiṣṭhānātsarvatraivaṁ bhaviṣyati||39||

EXPLANATION

When a person recognizes principle of spanda the basis of existence his awareness expands to infinite awareness he starts abiding in the self (yogi state). He will realize spanda is everywhere and abides in infinite awareness with all knowingness. To clarify further the limited being sheds the separate self and removes the veil (all states, vruttis, thoughts, ego, body-mind-intellect, perception-feeling-thought etc.). All knowing and experience happens in awareness and limited awareness expands to understand source as spanda. As spanda is everywhere, awareness yogi is also everywhere.

VERSE-40

ग्लानिर्विलुण्ठिका देहे तस्याश्चाज्ञानतः सृतिः।
तदुन्मेषविलुप्तं चेत्कुतः सा स्यादहेतुका॥॥

Glānirviluṇṭhikā dehe tasyāścājñānataḥ sṛtiḥ|
Tadunmeṣaviluptaṁ cetkutaḥ sā syādahetukā||40||

EXPLANATION

A person who is limited to body and mind is deprived of delight/bliss due to ignorance of the beauty of abiding in self. This depression (ignorance) is due to non-recognition of one's own nature of "self" (Satcchidananda). When unmesha (getting awake by opening eye lids) happens, this ignorance is destroyed. One finds his innate nature in bliss and happiness. The ignorance does not last to the awakened person. The yogi, though remains in body, is always abiding in "Self".

VERSE-41

एकचिन्ताप्रसक्तस्य यतः स्यादपरोदयः।
उन्मेषः स तु विज्ञेयः स्वयं तमुपलक्षयेत्॥॥

Ekacintāprasaktasya yataḥ syādaparodayaḥ|
Unmeṣaḥ sa tu vijñeyaḥ svayaṁ tamupalakṣayet||41||

EXPLANATION

This is a very important verse. When a yogi is in deep concentration of a thought or a particular matter or object, the mind is filled with focus. Then suddenly mind activities are numbed (slaying of the mind). Thought constructs disappear suddenly. Unmesha, a state of transcendental awareness is revealed with bliss swelling up and yogi experiences spanda principle directly. This bliss is unmesha. This is a realization, is not object, cannot be grasped but introspectively revealed to the yogi. Observe within oneself, realizing the big I consciousness without any effort. Unmesha is understood as the emergence of awareness in a person who is with one pointed focus. The awareness that, this awareness is himself, is the recognition of unmesha.

VERSE-42

अतो विन्दुरतो नादो रूपमस्मादतो रसः।
प्रवर्तन्तेऽचिरेणैव क्षोभकत्वेन देहिनः॥॥

Ato vindurato nādo rūpamasmādato rasaḥ|
Pravartante'cireṇaiva kṣobhakatvena dehinaḥ||42||

EXPLANATION

From this nada unmesha appears (light, sound, taste, form etc.) in a short time. These are sensory supernormal light, sound etc. The yogi who has realized self but still in identity with the body, gets a temporary satisfaction of senses, but are disturbing factors positively contributing to the yogi to move towards panda principle or fully abide in self. He continues introspection of unmesha through the identification of the body like above happens (taste, sound etc.). Ignores the supernatural stuffs as obstacles.

VERSE-43

दिदृक्षयेव सर्वार्थान्यदा व्याप्यावतिष्ठते।
तदा किं बहुनोक्तेन स्वयमेवावभोत्स्यते॥॥

Didṛkṣayeva sarvārthānyadā vyāpyāvatiṣṭhate|
Tadā kiṁ bahunoktena svayamevāvabhotsyate||43||

EXPLANATION

When a yogi abiding in infinite awareness of self, he sees the objects and outside world with his own light of consciousness. There is nothing more as everything of the outside world is in him. There is nothing more to explain as he will experience for himself the vision inside.

VERSE-44

प्रबुद्धः सर्वदा तिष्ठेज्ज्ञानेनालोक्य गोचरम्।
एकत्रारोपयेत्सर्वं ततोऽन्येन न पीड्यते॥॥

Prabuddhaḥ sarvadā tiṣṭhejjñānenālokya gocaram|
Ekatrāropayetsarvaṁ tato'nyena na pīḍyate||44||

EXPLANATION

The suprabuddha, (gnani, a realized one) is all the time awakened and mindful of all states of waking, sleeping and dreaming. Also, in Utpatti, Palana, Kama. Pralaya (creation, manifestation and dissolution). He sheds light of consciousness in every word, thought and thing. All the objects and world are all nothing but Shiva. The gnani, the suprabuddha, surrenders to this grace and lauds Shankara in that state of non-dual consciousness. This object, the seer, understands spanda principle and states there is no other but his own self. He is not troubled by anything separate. All is one and everything.

VERSE-45

शब्दराशिसमुत्थस्य शक्तिवर्गस्य भोग्यताम्।
कलाविलुप्तविभवो गतः सन्स पशुः स्मृतः॥॥

Śabdarāśisamutthasya śaktivargasya bhogyatām|
Kalāviluptavibhavo gataḥ sansa paśuḥ smṛtaḥ||45||

EXPLANATION

The verse requires deeper understanding. This is about an ignorance and separate self which makes a being limited and behaves like bound one (pashu). This happens due to Kala, the throw out, meaning happens to the limited activity in the outside world. The real nature of being non-dual Shiva the prakasha, the light that illumines. The non-dual Shiva through his swatantra does creation, manifestation and dissolution. Concealment (tirodhana) within bracket and Anugraha (grace). It is the perfect I-consciousness. The small I, ego-covered self is a limited being.

The I-consciousness of Shiva while in singularity with curiosity plays a "leela" with his freedom of swatantrya. He displays and manifests different forms on the screen of his own self. The I-consciousness (non-dual), manifests thus and in the diverse objects of the world. Cause - moving (vibrating) is spanda, the Throb. Thus, the Prakasha illuminating light of non-dual Shiva and his own reflection vimarsha form the seed (oval) and matrix (consonant) representing Shiva and Shakti. It further manifests into nine bold letters groups and 50 whole letters in these groups (shabda rashi). The divine non-dual I consciousness of Shiva is reduced to a bound limited being (Soul). How does this happen? This is due to Kala. The glory of Shiva consciousness is veiled by his own Maya (Kala vilupta vibhavaha). Kala means power supported by limited activity. The experient, (bound soul), does not rest in real self, even momentarily being attracted by the power groups and thus becomes bound. The real nature has not gone anywhere but he is not aware, he is deprived because of kalas and is outwardly consumed in vruttis, actions and words.

VERSE-46

परामृतरसापायस्तस्य यः प्रत्ययोद्भवः।
तेनास्वतन्त्रतामेति स च तन्मात्रगोचरः॥॥

Parāmṛtarasāpāyastasya yaḥ pratyayodbhavaḥ|
Tenāsvatantratāmeti sa ca tanmātragocaraḥ||46||

EXPLANATION

There is rise of ideas in the bound soul (Pashu) or limited self through the tanmatras (Shabda, Ganda, Rupa, Spasha, Rasa) act as a veil in the consciousness or self, thus obstructing the flow of bliss of immortality. The ideas can be of the world or bookish knowledge of spirituality. Though the infinite awareness of self is ever present, its presence is not recognized. This is due to feeding by the tanmatras to be occupied in the thoughts and actions outwardly. It has to be understood that in all states and in words, objects and thoughts, there is Shiva state everywhere. The limited being identifies only with separate self, thus missing the ever-presence of Shiva consciousness in him and in all things thoughts and words.

VERSE-47

स्वरूपावरणे चास्य शक्तयः सततोत्थिताः।
यतः शब्दानुवेधेन न विना प्रत्ययोद्भवः॥॥

Svarūpāvaraṇe cāsya śaktayaḥ satatotthitāḥ|
Yataḥ śabdānuvedhena na vinā pratyayodbhavaḥ||47||

EXPLANATION

The group of power are ready to veil the big I consciousness, (real nature). The ideas arise due to association of words. These ideas with power groups act to conceal the real nature of self, which is identical to Shiva. The ideas and concepts thus create veil and hide the real nature. Though this conditioning is also Shiva (the veil is also Shiva), the use of this veil to abide in Self is not possible if one is lost in the words and its web constituting ideas and concepts. By being aware of the real nature, one can break this veil and use it to abide in Shiva consciousness.

VERSE-48

सेयं क्रियात्मिका शक्तिः शिवस्य पशुवर्तिनी।
बन्धयित्री स्वमार्गस्था ज्ञाता सिद्ध्युपपादिका॥॥

Seyaṁ kriyātmikā śaktiḥ śivasya paśuvartinī|
Bandhayitrī svamārgasthā jñātā siddhyupapādikā||48||

EXPLANATION

Shiva the non-dual consciousness manifests as Shakti in the world and in limited self (of being). The I-consciousness of self which is infinite awareness as Shiva consciousness is bound by space and time and is activated as Kriya Shakti in the outer world. As this identity gets active in the outer world, it is a source of bondage (misery etc.). The operative power is still in the light of divine consciousness which gives rise to this bondage. Once the yogi recognizes the operating power in Shiva consciousness the veil drops, and the yogi attains bliss and peace of being the same as the infinite awareness (Shiva consciousness). He clearly sees Shakti as manifestation of Shiva and succeeds.

VERSE-49

तन्मात्रोदयरूपेण मनोऽहम्बुद्धिवर्तिना।
पुर्यष्टकेन संरुद्धस्तदुत्थं प्रत्ययोद्भवम्॥ ॥

Tanmātrodayarūpeṇa mano'hambuddhivartinā|
Puryaṣṭakena saṁruddhastadutthaṁ pratyayodbhavam||49||

VERSE-50

भुङ्क्ते परवशो भोगं तद्भावात्संसरेदतः।
संसृतिप्रलयस्यास्य कारणं सम्प्रचक्ष्महे॥ ॥

Bhuṅkte paravaśo bhogaṁ tadbhāvātsaṁsaredataḥ|
Saṁsṛtipralayasyāsya kāraṇaṁ sampracakṣmahe||50||

EXPLANATION

Puryashtaka is the experience that rises in the mind due to Tanmatras, plus Buddhi, Manas and Ahankara. These are concepts and ideas which emerges and drives the bound soul to external world and pleasures and sorrow. These ideas and concepts also drive the person to continuously engage in the outer world. This continues to future birth to carrying the puryasthaka. Thus, a repository is made of these concepts and desires. The bound soul goes through various births due to this trap of the limited being continuously bound to the externality of one. This is further explained in future verses.

VERSE-51

यदा त्वेकत्र संरूढस्तदा तस्य लयोदयौ।
नियच्छन्भोक्तृतामेति ततश्चक्रेश्वरो भवेत्॥॥

Yadā tvekatra saṁrūḍhastadā tasya layodayau|
Niyacchanbhoktṛtāmeti tataścakreśvaro bhavet||51||

EXPLANATION

When one abides in self and is rooted in Spanda principle, one can bring emergence and dissolution of Puryashtaka (which is referred to previous verse). Established in I-consciousness, he can bring the manifestation and dissolution of his world. Thus enters Shankara consciousness as described in the first verse. He therefore controls at will both inner world and outer world, outer world being universe, as Shiva himself. He does enjoy uninterrupted bliss and becomes one with Shiva himself.

This completes the Vibhuti Pada.

Chapter-4

PRAYER TO SPANDA STATE AND GURU

VERSE-52

अगाधसंशयाम्भोधिसमुत्तरणतारिणीम्।
वन्दे विचित्रार्थपदां चित्रां तां गुरुभारतीम्॥॥

Agādhasaṁśayāmbhodhisamuttaraṇatāriṇīm|
Vande vicitrārthapadāṁ citrāṁ tāṁ gurubhāratīm||52||

EXPLANATION

In this verse I pay homage to the guru who has delivered a supreme speech on spanda principle with “Para Vak” which has provided like a boat made of Spanda principle into words arranged in a way to cross the ocean of all doubts. In return I offer my prayer to Spanda immersed in supreme I consciousness.

VERSE-53

लब्ध्वाप्यलभ्यमेतज्ज्ञानधनं हृद्गुहान्तकृतनिहितेः।
वसुगुप्तवच्छिवाय हि भवति सदा सर्वलोकस्य॥॥

Labdhvāpyalabhyametajjñānadhanaṁ hṛdguhāntakṛtanihiteḥ|
Vasuguptavacchivāya hi bhavati sadā sarvalokasya||53||

EXPLANATION

This is the last verse of Spanda Karika. This treasure of knowledge was revealed to Vasugupta on the rocks. He kept it in the cave of his heart as attainment of his treasure. Heart is the light (prakasha), our consciousness and vimashra is awareness of this consciousness. It is like a cave. This is a treasure in the heart of Vasugupta. So, it will be for the good of all. There is no restriction on one to achieve this and preserve it. Just thus one enters the Shankara, the Shiva consciousness in the cave of heart, cave of heart and bring and spread good to all in the universe.